OLD LONDON BRIDGE LOST AND FOUND

Bruce Watson

English Heritage
Museum of London Archaeology Service

Dedication

This book is dedicated to the memory of Peter Jackson FSA, who died on 2 May 2003, aged 81. He was a great artist and illustrator, who brought London's history to life and produced some outstanding views of Roman and medieval London Bridge. Peter contributed 11 images to this publication and we are deeply indebted to him for his assistance with the production of the artwork for this publication.

Published in November 2004 by the Museum of London Archaeology Service

A CIP catalogue record for this book is available from the British Library

ISBN 1 901992 48 9

For a list of other MoLAS books visit the publications page at www.molas.org.uk

FRONT COVER: TOP Peter Jackson's depiction of medieval London Bridge in c 1400; BOTTOM London Bridge in 1909, a view looking westwards by H Marshall

INSIDE FRONT COVER Gordon Home's seven ages of London Bridge

RIGHT Royal Mail stamps produced in 2002, showing (from left) Millennium Bridge, Tower Bridge, Westminster Bridge, London Bridge (1647) and Blackfriars Bridge

Contents

Acknowledgements

The research and writing of this book was generously funded by English Heritage, who also provided a grant to cover the cost of publication.

Thanks to Gos Home, who generously offered us the use of his father Gordon's extensive collection of London Bridge material and the original artwork used in his 1931 publication, *Old London Bridge*, plus the painting of the 1633 fire (page 47); and to the late Peter Jackson for producing the view of the Vauxhall bridge (page 10) and for kindly allowing us to reproduce many other items of his original artwork.

The following institutions and individuals are thanked for their permission to reproduce the illustrations on the pages indicated: Ashmolean Museum, Oxford 44; The British Library 33; Trustees of the British Museum 35; British School at Rome 15; Dean and Chapter of Westminster Abbey 43; Ronald Embleton 13; Essex County Council/Nick Nethercoat 8; English Heritage/Judith Dobie 21; Peter Froste 7, 16; Derek Hewett for permission to reproduce the portrait of his ancestor Sir William Hewett 41; Gordon Home frontispiece, this page, 2, 3, 4, 28, 33, 34, 35, 36, 37, 39, 40, 41, 42, 46, 48, 49, 50, 51, 52, 53, 56, back cover; Guildhall Art Gallery, Corporation of London 53; Guildhall Library, Corporation of London 6, 38, 54; Herne Bay Record Society 55; Peter Jackson cover (top), 20, 23, 29, 30, 31; Lake Havasu City, Arizona 1, 57; Derek Lucas 11; The National Portrait Gallery, London 34, 38, 50; Norwegian Institute for Cultural Heritage Research/Birger R Lindstad (www.niku.no/olvasfro/english/1olvas.htm) 24; Andreas Pangerl (www.Romancoins.info) 17; John Pearson 18; Reading Museum Service 25; Rheinisches Landesmuseum Trier 15; Murray A Robertson 36; Royal Academy (1996 *Living Bridges Exhibition*)/Andy Chopping 46; Alan Sorrell 9; Richard Sorrell 14; Transport for London 57; US Fish and Wildlife Services www.fws.gov 8; The VRoma Project (www.vroma.org) 11; P Warner 16; The Worshipful Company of Fishmongers 54. The British Postage Stamps are reproduced by permission of Royal Mail.

Other photographs have been produced by MoLAS (Ryszard Bartkowiak 58, 59; Andy Chopping 2, 4, 8, 11, 13, 15, 16, 19, 20, 35, 37, 40, 42, 46, 57; Maggie Cox 13, 20, 26; Bruce Watson 18, 24, 27, 28, 39, 56, also illustration 24) and the Museum of London (Archaeological Archive 16; Photography Department 59; Picture Library cover (bottom), 9, 11, 13, 14, 16, 20, 22, 38, 42, 44, 47, 48, 49, 52, 53, 55, 56, 59). All other artwork was produced by the MoLAS Graphics team (Susan Banks, Neville Constantine, Jane Dunn and Sophie Lamb).

The text was edited by Sue Hirst, Peter Rowsome and Sue Wright. Reprographics by Andy Chopping; design and production by Tracy Wellman; printing by Linney Print.

ABOVE *Section of London Bridge balustrade reused at Herne Bay pier*

FOREWORD

Citizens of London will be pleased to know that Sir John Rennie's London Bridge continues to attract millions to its rather odd home in the American south-west. Many of its admirers are surprised to learn that this London Bridge is much more than just a tourist attraction and icon for a popular nursery school song; this bridge has several important functions that it serves with strength and grace.

In the mid 1960s, land developer and entrepreneur, Robert P McCulloch, was pursuing his vision of a resort community on the shore of picturesque Lake Havasu on the Colorado river. In the process, government authorities informed McCulloch that his project could not proceed without a plan to refresh river water that was stagnating downstream of a prominent peninsula. Undaunted, McCulloch devised a plan to correct the water quality problem using a mile-long channel dredged across the base of the peninsula, thereby severing Pittsburg Point and giving it a new name – The Island. An extraordinary island demands an extraordinary bridge and, as luck would have it, at almost that very moment in 1968, the City of London announced Rennie's bridge was for sale. McCulloch made the purchase and onlookers on both sides of the Atlantic watched in disbelief as the world-famous bridge was carefully dismantled stone by stone and shipped to America. It took four years and hundreds of craftsmen to painstakingly remove the facing from the huge granite blocks, and carefully and accurately return each one to its correct position on the surface of a concrete shell that was constructed to meet the demands of a modern, working bridge.

Even with its updated hollow core, we think Sir John Rennie would be pleased to know his bridge not only continues to carry people and traffic from one shore to another, it also serves to inspire and stir the imagination of all who experience its timeless beauty, history and grandeur along the way.

Robert G 'Bob' Whelan
Mayor, Lake Havasu City, Arizona USA

ABOVE Rennie's London Bridge in its new setting in Arizona

BELOW Bob Whelan

1

1 OLD LONDON BRIDGE REDISCOVERED

... the Thames is liquid history

British politician replying to an American who had compared the Thames disparagingly with the Mississippi, *Daily Mail* 25 Jan 1943

LEFT *View of modern London Bridge looking north, with the outline of the medieval bridge superimposed*

BELOW *View of old London Bridge in the 1920s looking south across the Thames from London Bridge Wharf, where the medieval bridge once stood*

How do you lose a huge medieval bridge?

We have all lost small objects, like our car keys, but to lose a large bridge sounds unlikely. Old London Bridge was 'lost' only in the sense of being lost from view on various occasions. Subsequently its below-ground remains have been rediscovered during redevelopment and their existence recorded by different generations of archaeologists. In central London the value of land has always ensured that any derelict buildings are soon swept away and their sites reused. Centuries of redevelopment have produced an accumulation of debris across central London during the past 2000 years, resulting in a city which is now literally built on its own history. A deeply buried Roman and medieval landscape exists, which archaeologists explore whenever the construction of new buildings and other developments threaten its destruction.

Early discoveries

Archaeological interest in London Bridge began in 1826–41, when the redundant medieval bridge was torn down and its site extensively dredged. A new bridge designed by John Rennie was opened in 1831. The demolition of the old bridge created a lot of public interest in its history, which resulted in the publication of *Chronicles of London Bridge* (1827). But it was the dredging around the site of the bridge that attracted most

archaeological interest because of the well-preserved metal finds it revealed, including thousands of Roman coins, a bronze head from a life-sized statue of the Roman Emperor Hadrian and two medieval wooden statues.

London Bridge returned to public attention in 1921 when one of the northern arches of the medieval bridge was discovered during the construction of Adelaide House. Sadly, despite public appeals that it should be retained *in situ* or dismantled stone by stone and rebuilt at the 1924 British Empire Exhibition at Wembley, nothing happened due to lack of money and it was demolished in October 1922. However, this discovery was

the inspiration for Gordon Home to start his wonderful book on the history of the bridge. Work on the site of Adelaide House is reputed to have produced a number of battleaxes, spearheads and a grappling iron all dating to about AD 1000.

In the period 1967–71 popular attention again focused on London Bridge, when Rennie's bridge was replaced. The Rennie bridge was sold to the McCulloch Oil Company, who rebuilt it stone by stone in 1968–71 at Lake Havasu City, Arizona, USA, as a tourist attraction. It was this rebuilding which inspired Peter Jackson to produce a pictorial history of the bridge.

LEFT The arch of medieval London Bridge discovered during the redevelopment of Adelaide Place, Daily Graphic, 14 July 1920

BELOW LEFT Diagram of the London Bridge arch discovered in 1921 at Adelaide Place

1176-1209
arch of original bridge

1703
ribs added

wooden
piles

1758
extension

1176-1209
bridge pier

1758
extension

ABOVE An 1827 reconstruction of medieval London Bridge showing how it might have looked in 1209 but incorrect without the houses which were built as an original feature

Recent finds

Systematic archaeological work on the northern end of the bridgehead began during 1979, when the development of various derelict warehouses and redundant office blocks commenced, and work continued intermittently until 1996. These excavations revealed the timber quays of the Roman port and fragments of Roman London bridge.

The redevelopment of the site of the southern end of the bridge, the Southwark bridge abutment (now known as No. 1 London Bridge), during 1984 revealed the medieval bridge abutment, its contemporary waterfronts and the buildings which lined its approach road. But most importantly, below the medieval abutment were the well-preserved remains of a succession of earlier Saxo-Norman timber bridges. It was these discoveries, and those of the Roman bridge on the opposite side of the Thames, which prompted a reassessment of the history of Roman and medieval London Bridge.

Now the Corporation of London manages London Bridge, along with the City of London's other road bridges and the Millennium Bridge. The surplus monies from Bridge House Estates, which formerly maintained London Bridge, have since 1995 been used by the Bridge House Trust Fund to finance a variety of charitable projects for the benefit of Londoners. The records of the Bridge House estate, which date back to 1381, give us a unique window on the maintenance of the medieval bridge.

LEFT Excavations at Fennings Wharf, Southwark, in 1984 showing upstanding masonry of the west side of the 15th-century bridge

RIGHT The symbol of Bridge House Estates

BELOW Excavating the Saxo-Norman bridge revetments

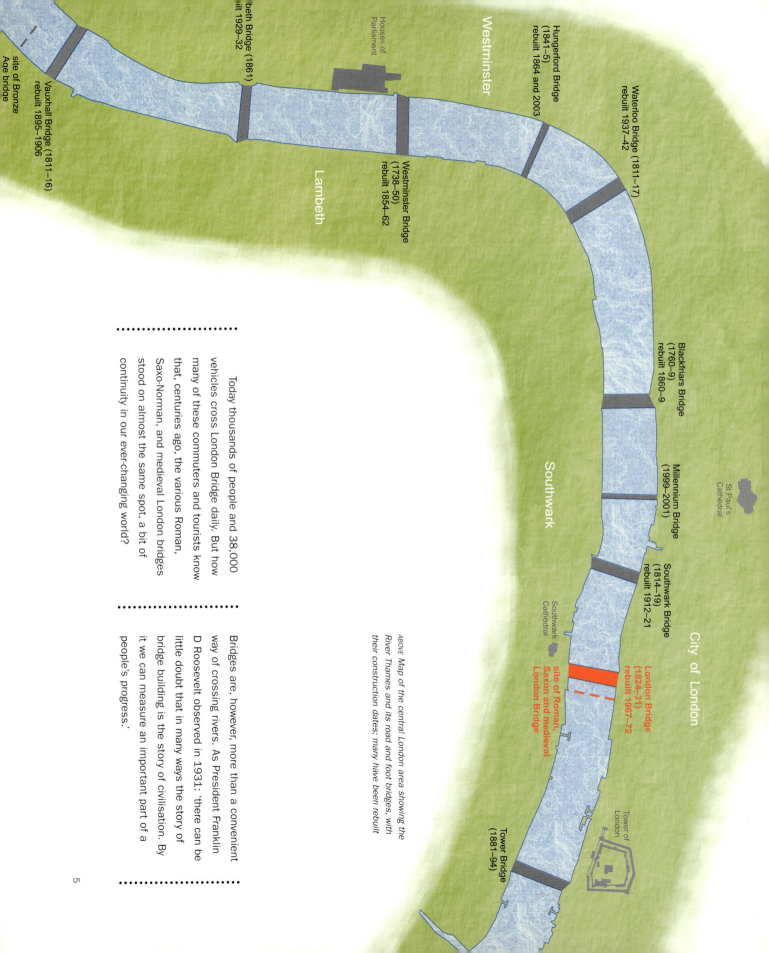

site of Bronze
Age bridge

Vauxhall Bridge (1811–16)
rebuilt 1895–1906

beth Bridge
ilt 1929–32

Houses of
Parliament

Westminster

Lambeth

eth Bridge (1861)

Westminster Bridge
(1738–50)
rebuilt 1854–62

Hungerford Bridge
(1841–5)
rebuilt 1864 and 2003

Waterloo Bridge (1811–17)
rebuilt 1937–42

St Paul's
Cathedral

Blackfriars Bridge
(1760–9)
rebuilt 1860–9

Millennium Bridge
(1999–2001)

Southwark Bridge
(1814–19)
rebuilt 1912–21

City of London

Southwark

Southwark
Cathedral

**site of Roman,
Saxon and medieval
London Bridge**

**London Bridge
(1824–31)
rebuilt 1967–72**

Tower of
London

Tower Bridge
(1881–94)

ABOVE Map of the central London area showing the River Thames and its road and foot bridges, with their construction dates; many have been rebuilt

Today thousands of people and 38,000 vehicles cross London Bridge daily. But how many of these commuters and tourists know that, centuries ago, the various Roman, Saxo-Norman, and medieval London bridges stood on almost the same spot, a bit of continuity in our ever-changing world?

Bridges are, however, more than a convenient way of crossing rivers. As President Franklin D Roosevelt observed in 1931: 'there can be little doubt that in many ways the story of bridge building is the story of civilisation. By it we can measure an important part of a people's progress.'

2 THE PREHISTORIC THAMES

Flow sweet river flow,
Sweet Thames flows softly
Chorus to traditional song

ABOVE *Rocque's 1746 map of the Isle of Dogs, showing a breach in the river walls; from the 17th century onwards windmills (circled) were built on the west part of the river walls to lift water from the drainage channels into the river*

The trailing Thames

To Londoners today, the Thames is just the blue bit in their A to Zs, restrained by concrete walls and with the Thames Barrier to stop it flooding the capital. To see the Thames as a natural river today you have to travel upstream to Oxfordshire, where it still flows past meadows, which it can flood when the water level rises. The prehistoric Thames was much broader and shallower than the modern river and it sprawled across a large, low-lying marshy floodplain. In parts of east London such as the Isle of Dogs, the flood plain was so low-lying that it remained uninhabited marshland until the 18th century, when it was only reclaimed by the building of massive river walls. In Southwark the naturally low-lying topography consisted of sand and gravel islands (the focus of early settlement) surrounded by a network of tidal creeks, streams and marshes. Parts of Bermondsey in east Southwark were not drained or adequately protected by river walls until the 18th century and not built over until later. Today the Thames is tidal up to Richmond lock but the tidal head of the river during the Bronze Age was Westminster.

The very low-lying nature of many portions of the Thames flood plain, such as Southwark or the Isle of Dogs, means that these are some of the first parts of central London to suffer from the effects of rising sea level or marine transgressions. This has resulted in these areas being repeatedly flooded and thick layers of clay sediments being laid down. These periodic transgressions are mainly caused by global warming, melting the polar ice sheets, which causes the sea level to rise. Since the 3rd century AD there has been a sustained transgression, the rate of which is now accelerating, hence the need for the Thames Barrier to stop London from flooding.

ABOVE View looking north-west across the prehistoric Thames before the foundation of London; later London bridge spanned the river from the island in the lower centre to the north bank (upper right)

The Thames as a resource and a religious focus

The prehistoric Thames was a great resource, a routeway, a barrier and also a shrine. The Thames and its adjoining marshlands would have been a great economic resource for both fishing and wild fowling, while the marshlands could also provide seasonal pasture. For centuries people have been constructing fish traps along the shallow margins of the Thames. A fish trap of either Bronze Age or Iron Age date has been discovered on the Thames foreshore at Vauxhall. However, most of the surviving examples of Thames fish traps are of Saxon (AD 410–900) or later date.

Until the Thames became grossly polluted during the early 19th century, it was teeming with many species of fish. Since 1957, when the entire tidal river was officially described as 'virtually lifeless', the water quality has greatly improved thanks to the proper treatment of sewage and the ceaseless efforts of the Environment Agency; the river is now home to over 115 species of fish including salmon.

As a routeway the Thames offers easy access into central England, facilitating trade and transport but vulnerable to invasion. Downstream of Westminster the river also functioned as a barrier, which could only be crossed by boat, as the water would have been too deep and the river bed too muddy to wade across.

ABOVE Roman stone head of bearded deity found in Southwark; interpreted as a river god

LEFT Reconstuction of an 8th-century AD Saxon fish weir from the Blackwater estuary, Essex; traditional design consisting of a V-shaped brushwood structure which channelled the fish into a central basket; prehistoric examples were probably of a similar design

BELOW Atlantic salmon

© Essex County Council

It is clear that our ancestors venerated the Thames, as numerous Neolithic (4000–2000 BC) flint tools and Bronze Age (2000–600 BC) weapons have been recovered during dredging. This material is interpreted as votive offerings made to the spirit of the river. During the Iron Age (600 BC to AD 43) people carried on throwing treasure into the Thames – finds recovered during dredging include a splendid horned helmet and the beautiful Battersea shield (on display in the British Museum). Some of these votive artefacts are on display in the prehistoric gallery of the Museum of London. As water is a requirement of daily life and floods can cause great loss of life, the worship of springs and rivers as a source of both life and death has occurred within many cultures. Today some people push supermarket trolleys into rivers and canals, an action that most believe to be the efforts of hooligans not an act of worship, but one that future archaeologists might interpret as part of our worship of shopping.

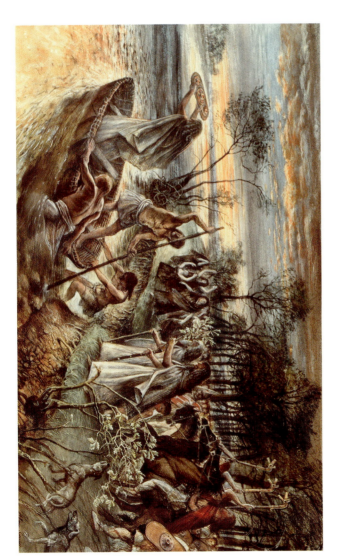

ABOVE Prehistoric oak stave and bronze communal drinking vessel found in the Thames

LEFT Early 1st-century AD bronze parade shield with glass inlay from Battersea

BELOW Artist's reconstruction of the ceremony of casting the shield into the Thames

The Bronze Age bridge at Vauxhall

It is probable that the first bridge to be built over part of the Thames at Vauxhall was constructed for religious or ritual reasons during the Bronze Age. The Vauxhall bridge was discovered during the archaeological survey of the Thames foreshore in 1993 and its timbers have been radiocarbon-dated (see Glossary) to about 1550 BC. The structure consists of two lines of eroded vertical posts driven into the foreshore; these apparently supported trestles, which were further anchored by angled struts. It is assumed that the decking was in turn suspended between the trestles. The full length of the structure is uncertain but the surviving portion of it is over 15m long. It is interpreted as a bridge linking the south bank of the Thames to a small island in midstream, which was lost to erosion long ago. This tiny island was probably too low-lying to live on and it seems unlikely that a bridge was constructed just to enable livestock grazing on the island. The presence of two complete Bronze Age spearheads found near the site of the bridge suggests that they were votive offerings not accidental losses. It is possible that the Vauxhall bridge

Reconstruction of Vauxhall Bronze Age bridge, view looking north

provided access to an island which was used for the disposal of the dead. Corpses could have been disposed of on the island by exposure or excarnation. Until the mid 19th century the Sioux Plains Indians exposed their dead fully clothed on platforms or in trees for one year before burial. In parts of the modern world 'water burial' is still practised, so it is possible that this method of disposal was used here during the prehistoric period. It is common practice in Laos to scatter people's ashes into local rivers, while the Hindus take the remains of their deceased to the River Ganges for disposal.

The excavation of the Southwark medieval bridge abutment in 1984 revealed a circular Bronze Age ditch (a 'ring ditch') on the nearby foreshore. Within the backfills of the ditch and the central feature were spreads of ash and cremated human bone, probably derived from the scattering of debris from nearby cremation fires. Radiocarbon dates show that the ring ditch was used as a cremation cemetery from about 1900–1600 BC. After this it was buried by fluvial clays, the result of prolonged flooding caused by another phase of marine transgression.

The name of the River Thames provides another link with our prehistory, as it was in

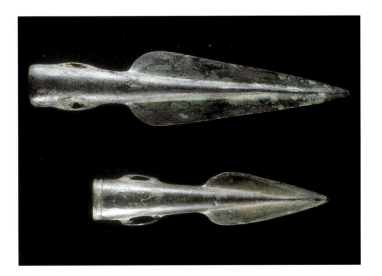

use over 2000 years ago. Julius Caesar, during his second invasion of Britain in 54 BC, first described it as the *Tamesis*, presumably drawing on local knowledge. The origin of this river name is uncertain. It may be derived from the same linguistic route as

other English river names such as the Tams or Teme, meaning 'dark river' (one with water discoloured by sediment). However, more recent research suggests that the Thames is one of a number of river names based on the root *ta* or *te* meaning to flow.

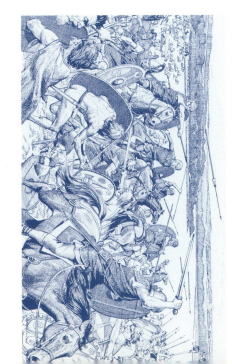

LEFT Bust of Julius Caesar, soldier and statesman, murdered 44 BC

FAR LEFT The Bronze Age spearheads found near the Vauxhall bridge

BELOW Caesar's invading army clashing with native warriors on the banks of the Thames in 54 BC

3 ROMAN LONDON BRIDGE

Roman roads

Urban London starts with the Romans, as the place was effectively a 'green field site' before they arrived. Roman London or Londinium only developed as a port and a major urban centre because of the Thames. It was here at London, where the river channel narrowed, that the Romans decided to bridge the river. The site was clearly carefully chosen, as the bridge approach roads were sited on natural promontories on each bank, thus avoiding the necessity to construct causeways across the floodplain and making the task of bridging easier. Roman London was an important road junction, where Watling Street, running west from the Kent ports, converged with Staine Street running north from Chichester. It is certain that the roads on each side of the Thames were intended to be linked by a bridge and an original bridge, possibly not intended as permanent, may have been built c AD 50. Alternatively a ferry may have connected the two roads at first.

The Roman army were great builders of roads and bridges. For instance, Julius Caesar in 55 BC had a temporary wooden bridge constructed by his engineers in only ten days. This feat allowed him to move his army across to the east bank of the Rhine at Koblenz to carry out a punitive raid on some unfortunate German tribe. Doubtless

On learning the enemy's plan of campaign, Caesar led his army to the Thames in order to enter Cassivellaunus' territory. The river is fordable at one point only, and even there with difficulty. At this place he found large enemy forces drawn up on the opposite bank ... He sent the cavalry across first, and then ordered the infantry to follow ...

Caesar, The Conquest of Gaul, *describing his crossing of the Thames during his second invasion of Britain in 54 BC*

Caesar's engineers had been stockpiling materials for this project for months, but it is an impressive feat even by modern standards to span a river some 360m wide and up to 7m deep in such a short time.

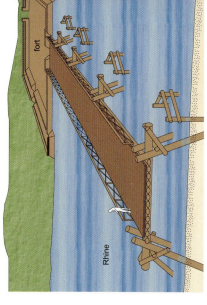

ABOVE *Reconstruction diagram of Caesar's bridge across the Rhine*

LEFT *Map of the Roman road network in south-east England*

In AD 63–4, shortly after the destruction of Roman London by the followers of the rebel Queen Boudica in AD 60, the Roman army built London's first port facility: a massive oak baulk quay on either side of the north (City of London) bridgehead. Perhaps they replaced or repaired a first London Bridge or again ran a ferry service. The intention of the Roman army was probably first to rebuild infrastructure as we do today after disasters. A new bridge would have

allowed the Roman army to bring aid for the civil population and to move their own equipment and supplies. This new port was clearly a success and it was the commercial growth of London that ensured that the Romans chose it as the provincial capital. The importance and wealth of London would have doubtless ensured that it possessed an imposing bridge, which would also have served as a visual symbol of imperial power and authority.

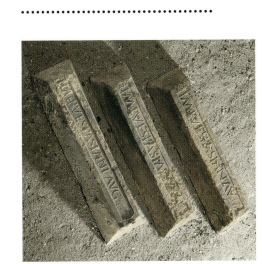

LEFT Riverside face of mid 1st-century quay at Regis House on the north bank of the Thames

ABOVE RIGHT Three lead ingots from the Mendips bearing the stamp of the Emperor Vespasian AD 69–79; found in a quayside building on the north bank close to the bridge

RIGHT Reconstruction of 1st-century port on the north bank with the north pier of the bridge behind

Roman London bridge

Archaeological excavations at the south end of Fish Street in 1981 revealed part of a massive timber structure interpreted as part of a temporary timber bridge, built about AD 85–90. This structure was superseded in the period AD 90–120 by a permanent bridge built alongside it. This new bridge had a massive landward masonry abutment most of which still lies deeply buried under the junction of Fish Street Hill with Lower Thames Street. Our knowledge of this bridge is fragmentary, but it is believed to have been about 340m long. It was founded on deeply seated, diamond-shaped, brick-built piers, infilled with clay and rubble, which supported a wooden superstructure of decking with handrails. It probably looked similar to the Apollodorus bridge depicted on Trajan's column or the surviving Roman bridge at Trier, in Germany. As the Roman port developed

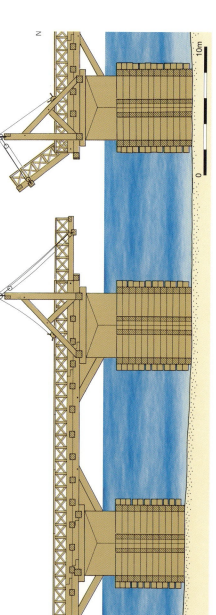

ABOVE Reconstruction of the building of the late 1st-century timber Roman London bridge

LEFT Reconstructed elevation of the final phase of Roman London bridge

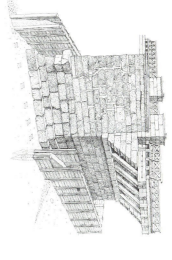

both up- and downstream of the bridge, there was presumably some sort of drawbridge to allow boats to sail through.

Altars dedicated to the sea gods Oceanus and Neptune are known from the site of the Roman bridge spanning the Tyne at Newcastle-upon-Tyne. These finds suggest that the Tyne bridge possessed some sort of temple or shrine, where sailors could either give thanks for a safe return or make offerings to the gods before setting sail. The tiny representation of a Roman galley prow recovered from the river near the site of the permanent Roman

London bridge is likely to be a votive offering. The presence of a shrine or temple on Roman London bridge would explain why thousands of coins, some of which are bent or broken, and various small figurines of Roman gods were showered into the Thames in one particular spot, according to Charles Roach Smith, who collected many of these finds from the men who were doing the dredging. The link between bridges and places of worship continued during the medieval period when many urban bridges, including London Bridge, possessed chapels.

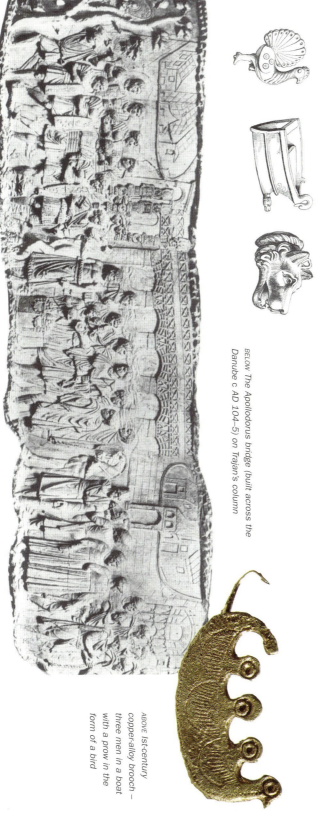

ABOVE Reconstruction drawing of a pier of the Roman bridge at Trier, Germany; the actual reconstruction of the bridge at Trier incorrectly has stone not wooden arches

BELOW FROM LEFT Roman figure of a peacock; bronze model of Roman galley prow; Roman steelyard weight in the form of a dog's head; all from the Thames near the site of Roman London bridge

BELOW The Apollodorus bridge (built across the Danube c AD 104–5) on Trajan's column

ABOVE 1st-century copper-alloy brooch – three men in a boat with a prow in the form of a bird

Other Roman finds recovered by dredging include the imposing life-sized bronze head of Emperor Hadrian (reigned AD 117–38). Perhaps the head was part of a civic monument on the bridge, which might have been erected to commemorate his visit to Britain during AD 122. The statue may have been torn down during one of the later insurrections that affected Roman Britain. Hadrian was apparently a popular emperor but rebels could have seen his image as a symbol of Roman rule. In AD 286 or 287 the commander of the Roman channel fleet, Carausius, declared himself emperor and apparently made London his capital. Imperial authority was not re-established until AD 296.

During the 2003 Iraq war, the numerous statues of Saddam Hussein in the cities captured by the coalition forces were pulled down and broken up as a public demonstration of the end of the dictator's reign.

Roman London only acquired its landward walls in about AD 200, but the walls did not extend along the river frontage because of the need for unhindered access to the quays and wharves. The Roman bridge, like the medieval bridge, presumably served as part of the city's southern defences and controlled upstream access. Only after the port had largely gone out of use was the river frontage defended by a masonry wall, constructed in AD 255–75.

ABOVE *The 3rd-century river wall under construction*

BELOW *Roman London in the early 2nd century AD, looking upstream, showing the final phase of the Roman bridge with the amphitheatre, fort and public baths on the north bank (right)*

LEFT *Bronze head of Hadrian recovered from the Thames*

BELOW *Left hand and forearm of a gilded bronze Roman statue being conserved; the statue was broken up in c AD 70 and this part thrown into a pond (found in excavations at Blossom's Inn, London)*

4 THE END OF ROMAN LONDON BRIDGE

Roman London in decline

Roman London Bridge clearly would have been an important point in the communications network of south-east England. Perhaps it survived the demise of other public works in London during the 4th century. It would, however, be quite expensive to maintain the timber decking so, in the absence of effective regional government, the bridge may soon have become unusable. The number of Roman coins that were being thrown into the river sharply declined after AD 330, which could be interpreted as evidence of the bridge's demise. Alternatively it is possible that, following Emperor Constantine's edict of AD 313 tolerating the Christian faith, the pagan practice of throwing money into the river declined in popularity. Clearly a few people were still crossing the river by either bridge or ferry during the reign of Emperor Honorius (AD 395–423) and throwing in a few coins.

It is clear that by the 4th century AD both the economic and political importance of

London and Southwark was in decline. The walled city was apparently abandoned by the beginning of the 5th century. Britain at this time was under attack from the Scots (then known as the Picts), Irish and Germanic peoples. In AD 410 the Romans decided not to defend their frontier province any more and all their remaining military units were withdrawn from Britain. Honorius instructed the Britons to organise their own defences: an ignominious end to over 360 years of imperial rule.

Roman coinage went out of circulation and was hoarded on a large scale instead, perhaps for reasons of security or possibly because it could no longer be spent. With a breakdown of central Roman government and the money economy, regional trade could only have happened on a small scale, so there would have been much less road traffic and there would have been no authority or reason to maintain London bridge and the link to a now deserted city.

ABOVE Gold solidus of Honorius

17

Land-hungry Germanic immigrants (Angles, Saxons, Frisians and Jutes) settled in east England, including the Greater London area, from the 5th century onwards. These soldiers and settlers moved west along the Thames and its tributaries quickly establishing political control over the lands they occupied. According to the *Anglo-Saxon chronicle* in AD 449 a group of Germanic Saxons led by Hengest and Horsa landed at Ebbsfleet (Pegwell Bay) in east Kent to help the Britons but then mutinied and quickly conquered the area. In AD 456 the defeated Britons sought refuge in the

'stronghold of London'. Bishop Mellitus arrived in London in AD 604 and is believed to have founded a cathedral on the site of St Paul's. From this date onwards there presumably was a small community of priests and monks living inside the derelict Roman city.

BELOW Artist's impression of Roman London in the 5th century after a short period of abandonment, showing the crumbling riverside wall and collapsed bridge piers in the foreground

RIGHT Replica 'Viking' longship constructed in 1949 to commemorate the landing of Hengist and Horsa at Pegwell Bay, Kent, in AD 449

5 KING ALFRED AND THE SAXON BRIDGE

The remains of the Roman bridge were clearly not a hindrance to navigation, as from about AD 600 a Saxon settlement known as Lundenwic developed in the Strand area of modern Westminster, upstream of the bridge. According to the *Anglo-Saxon chronicle*, this wealthy undefended trading settlement was sacked by seafaring Scandinavian or Viking raiders from AD 842 onwards. These raids drove the inhabitants of Lundenwic to seek safety within the walls of the derelict Roman city. King Alfred (reigned AD 871–99) ordered the refortification of London in AD 886 as part of his strategy of fortress building to secure his territory and its navigable rivers against the Viking raiders. It has been suggested that the Thames was fortified by the rebuilding of the bridge during the 9th century, but there is no documentary or archaeological evidence for the existence of a bridge at this time. The importance of a well-defended bridge and associated landward defences was demonstrated by the

siege of Paris in AD 885–6. After a siege of some four months, the Vikings had failed to capture the Seine bridges and in desperation hauled their boats overland to bypass Paris, so they could continue upstream.

Viking raids

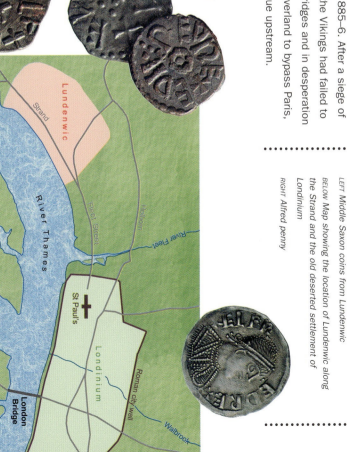

In this year there was great slaughter in London (Lundenwic), and in Cantwic (Canterbury), and in Rochester

Viking raids recorded in the *Anglo-Saxon chronicle* for AD 842

LEFT Middle Saxon coins from Lundenwic

BELOW Map showing the location of Lundenwic along the Strand and the old deserted settlement of Londinium

RIGHT Alfred penny

Lundenwic

Strand

River Thames

Fleet Street

Holborn

River Fleet

St Paul's

Londinium

Roman city wall

London Bridge

Walbrook

0   1km

The reoccupation of London

London was not simply refounded as a fortress. A port was established at Queenhithe (upstream of the bridge) and gradually the whole waterfront was lined with quays. A mint was established and the street grid we see today was developed to link the port to the main shopping centre and market along Cheapside. But then, in September AD 994, London was captured and burnt down by the Vikings. It is possible that this disaster prompted the rebuilding of London bridge and the fortification of the Southwark bridgehead, since the *Anglo-Saxon chronicle* records that subsequent raids failed to capture London. The existence of a new London bridge was first documented *c* AD 1000.

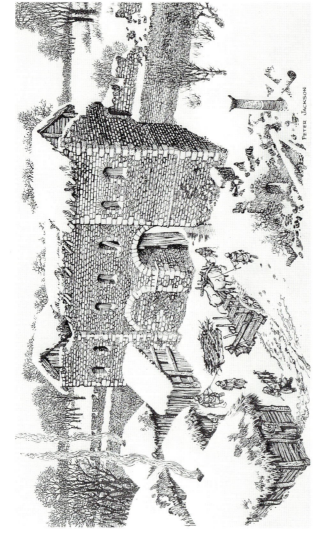

PETER JACKSON

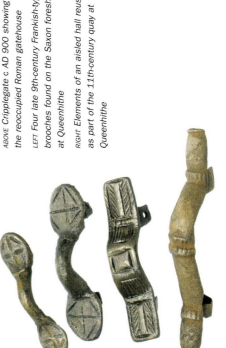

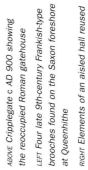

ABOVE *Cripplegate c AD 900 showing the reoccupied Roman gatehouse*

LEFT *Four late 9th-century Frankish-type brooches found on the Saxon foreshore at Queenhithe*

RIGHT *Elements of an aisled hall reused as part of the 11th-century quay at Queenhithe*

20

The rebuilding of London bridge

The archaeological evidence for the first Saxo-Norman London bridge consists of two water-logged oak timbers dated by dendrochronology (tree-ring dating) to *c* AD 987–1032. Neither of the timbers was in its original position. The first was a large squared log beam that was probably part of the foundations of the bridge abutment, but was found buried in fluvial silts, where the current had dropped it. The second timber was a smaller beam found reused as part of a later bridge structure. These timbers are interpreted as part of the late 10th- or early 11th-century bridge abutment destroyed by floods, ice flows or tidal scouring, which scattered its timbers along the Thames foreshore. Although the superstructure of the bridge is unknown, the development of the Saxo-Norman port both up- and downstream of the bridge implies that sea-going vessels could pass through it, presumably by means of a drawbridge

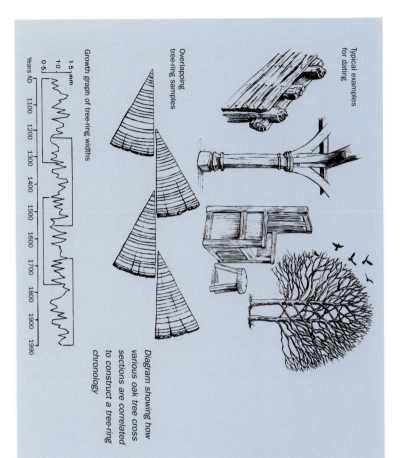

Typical examples for dating

Overlapping tree-ring samples

Growth graph of tree-ring widths

Diagram showing how various oak tree cross sections are correlated to construct a tree-ring chronology

Dendrochronology or tree-ring analysis is an important method of dating waterlogged oak or beech timbers found on archaeological sites. It works on the principle that deciduous trees produce an annual growth ring, the size of which is determined by fluctuations in temperature and rainfall. Study of these growth rings has allowed them to be dated by cross-matching them with other samples. If bark is present on a sample, then the precise year when the tree was felled can be determined. Often no bark survives due to carpentry and then the felling date of the oak timbers is estimated from the number of sapwood rings which lie below the bark and encircle the hardwood. Beech trees do not produce a band of sapwood.

6 BLOOD, FIRE AND ICE: EVENTS ON THE SAXON BRIDGE

Yet you broke the bridge of London,
Stout-hearted warrior,
You succeeded in conquering the land,
Iron swords made headway,
Strongly urged to conflict;
Ancient shields were broken,
Battle's fury mounted

Medieval Icelandic poet in praise of King Olaf's attack on London Bridge, quoted in the *Heimskringla* (written before c 1235)

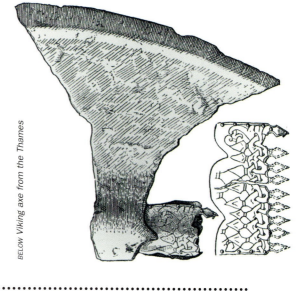

BELOW Viking axe from the Thames

The Vikings attack London bridge

England 1000 years ago was a troubled kingdom. King Ethelred 'the Unready' (AD 978–1016) was unable to defeat the powerful Viking armies, who by 1013 had conquered most of south-east England apart from London. The Londoners, fearful for their own safety, decided to surrender to the Viking leader Swein Forkbeard, King of Denmark, and Ethelred went into exile. After Swein's death in February 1014, Ethelred staged a comeback. But London was loyal to Swein's heir, his second son Cnut. According to the Olaf sagas, King Ethelred sought the help of Viking mercenaries to recapture London and regain his throne. London bridge was defended by forces loyal to Cnut, so a number of Viking ships led by Olaf Haraldsson and fitted with protective canopies (to protect the crews from missiles) sailed west upstream to the bridge. Despite the best efforts of the defending forces, the attackers managed to attach grappling irons and ropes to the bridge, then sailed

downstream and pulled down or badly damaged the bridge superstructure, compelling its defenders to surrender London to Ethelred. The Londoners' decision to surrender may have been prompted by the realisation that the forces defending the Southwark bridgehead could not have been supplied or reinforced from the north side of the river if the bridge was unusable.

After the recapture of London, Ethelred's fortunes improved. When the Viking army was defeated in Lindsey, Lincolnshire, Cnut was forced into exile, leaving Ethelred undisputed ruler of England. In 1016 Cnut returned to England with a large army to take his revenge. Shortly after Cnut's arrival Ethelred died in London 'worn out' by years of 'great toil and difficulties', according to the *Anglo-Saxon chronicle*. The succession to the English throne was disputed – Londoners wanted Ethelred's son Edmund to rule, but others preferred Cnut. In May 1016 Cnut's forces attempted to sail up the Thames, but

they were unable to capture London bridge and were forced to drag their ships overland across north Southwark to continue upstream. The matter of the succession to the English throne was decided on 30 November 1016 by Edmund's sudden death, an event that made Cnut the Great the undisputed king of England until his own death in 1035. Some of the iron battleaxes, spearheads and a grappling iron (on display in the Museum of London) found on the site of the bridge during the 1920s redevelopment might have been lost during these battles.

BELOW Artist's impression of the Viking attack on London bridge in 1014

Southwark after the battle of Hastings. They found the southern bridgehead defended against them and, having failed to capture it, burnt down the rest of Southwark in reprisal. William's army marched west and crossed the Thames further upstream, but returned to London in December 1066. William needed to capture London to secure his position as king, as it was the largest and richest English city. His forces apparently entered the city from the west and captured it after a battle within the walls. Having captured London, William immediately began to build the Tower of London and two other fortresses, known as Montfichet's Tower and Baynard's Castle. Both lay inside the city walls and were intended to ensure the loyalty of Londoners.

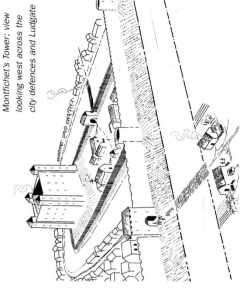

BELOW Reconstruction of Montfichet's Tower; view looking west across the city defences and Ludgate

St Olaf, the hero of London bridge

Olaf Haraldsson, the hero of the attack on London bridge, had returned home to Norway to become king in 1016; he ruled until 1029, when he was driven into exile. The following year Olaf died at the battle of Stiklestad while attempting to regain his throne. After Olaf's death Cnut ruled Norway. Olaf was buried at Trondheim, where miracles began to occur which led to his canonisation. His popularity as a saint was greatly boosted by the widespread hatred of

Cnut's son Swein, who ruled Norway as his father's regent. After Cnut's death in 1035 the Norwegians asked Olaf's son Magnus 'the good' to be their king. St Olaf was a popular saint in England as well as Norway – three medieval London churches were dedicated to him. The church that stood at the southern end of the bridge was also dedicated to him. The existence of a church here was first documented in 1096; it was rebuilt in 1740 and finally demolished in 1926. The site of the church is now an imposing art deco office block called 'St Olaf's House'.

London bridge was the scene of more conflict in 1066 when Duke William of Normandy and his victorious army arrived in

LEFT St Olaf distributes money before the battle of Stiklestad in 1030; reconstruction of a late 13th- or early 14th-century altar frontal

RIGHT St Olaf's House, Tooley Street, Southwark, on the site of the church (completed 1931)

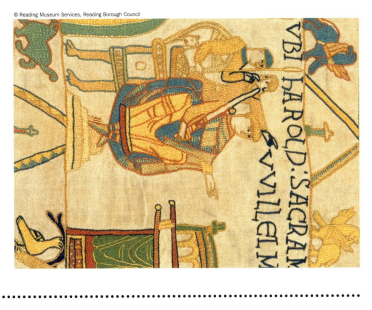

ABOVE Seated figure of William I as seen on the Bayeux tapestry

London bridge washes away

The second rebuilding of Saxo-Norman London bridge was represented archaeologically by a single massive horizontal oak timber. This timber formed part of the north side of a three-sided wooden structure, which was part of the late 11th- or early 12th-century bridge abutment foundations. This wooden box would have been infilled with clay or rubble, open on the south or landward side. Here there would have been a ramp to allow access up onto the bridge roadway, which must have been kept clear of high tides, floods and ice flows that would otherwise have been constantly washing it away. Cut into the top of this timber were two vertical slots, 4.6m apart, intended to support the superstructure of the abutment. These give us a good idea of the width of the bridge roadway. The Olaf sagas describe the 11th-century London bridge as 'so broad that two wagons could pass each other upon it'. The rest of what was undoubtedly an impressive structure seems to have been washed away or salvaged for reuse, leaving no trace.

In 1097 the *Anglo-Saxon chronicle* recorded that floods had carried away nearly all the bridge and that men employed in constructing the Tower of London and Westminster Hall, were sent to repair the

ABOVE Plan of Southwark bridgehead foreshore showing the second phase of the Saxo-Norman bridge abutment

bridge. This shows how important the bridge was, as labour was taken from two of King William's most prestigious projects to repair it. At about the same time that the bridge was washed away, the gravel foreshore upstream of the bridge was also suffering badly from erosion caused by the scouring of the tides and the effect of floods. This erosion would eventually have removed the bridge approach road and undermined the bridge abutment. To counter this threat clay and log banks were constructed, and lines of stakes hammered into the shore, backed by

laid horizontal planks and an artificial bank to consolidate the eroding foreshore. It must have been grim work for the unfortunate labourers – wading around the muddy Thames foreshore hammering in stakes or carrying baskets of clay – and the *Anglo-Saxon chronicle* noted that on such construction projects 'many a man was afflicted [suffered greatly]'.

These revetment structures were repeatedly destroyed by the river. Repairs were sometimes rushed and on one occasion the trunk of a plum tree was used,

perhaps felled in a local orchard or garden in the hurry to obtain materials. At the same time domestic rubbish was being dumped on the foreshore. Food waste included the bones of cattle, sheep/goat, chicken, goose, mallard, cod and whiting. Also present were the bones of a goshawk used in falconry, the sport of the rich.

The timber bridge was rebuilt yet again during the late 11th or early 12th century. Once again very little of the bridge survived and the only evidence of it was the timber foundation of the abutment.

LEFT *View to north from the Southwark foreshore of line of collapsed 11th-century revetment piles, evidence of the destruction of the revetment*

BELOW *Timber riverside revetment built c 1045 at Queenhithe to protect the shoreline from erosion*

London bridge rebuilt

Sometime in the mid 12th century the technique used to build and rebuild the bridge changed. Instead of the three-sided abutments, rectangular four-sided boxes or caissons were constructed in a log cabin style from horizontal oak timbers. The original caisson was rebuilt during 1160–78 according to tree-ring dating and this later phase was the most complete of all the timber bridge structures to survive. The caisson measured 5.1m north–south by about 6.0m east–west, which implies that the roadway it carried was no more than 6m wide. The problem of the erosion of the upstream foreshore was solved by constructing a series of heavy timber revetments or breakwaters aligned north–south to break the force of the tides and floods. Some of these revetments also helped support the

upstream side of the earth and rubble ramp that carried the approach road up to the top of the caisson. The approach road to the bridge was probably lined with small wooden thatched houses by this time.

No one really knows what the earlier Saxo-Norman bridges looked like, as the evidence lay outside areas that archaeologists could get at or simply did not survive. The only clue to the appearance of these bridges is a brief description of the 11th-century bridge in the sagas of St Olaf. These sagas describe the bridge superstructure as being made of 'vertical timber poles', which implies that it was of trestle construction with a plank or split log roadway and might have looked similar to the central portion of the 18th-century Whitney-on-Wye toll bridge.

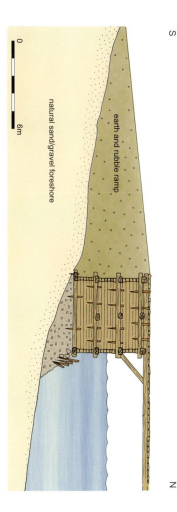

BELOW *Reconstructed elevation of the later phase of the 12th-century bridge caisson*

S

natural sand/gravel foreshore

earth and rubble ramp

N

0   6m

TOP *Plan of the later phase of the 12th-century bridge caisson and associated upstream revetment*

ABOVE *Whitney-on-Wye toll bridge, Herefordshire*

N

bridge

road

caisson

0   10m

7 BUILDING THE STONE BRIDGE

Why build a stone bridge?

Building a stone bridge is considerably more expensive than building a timber one, but the result is generally much more durable. Medieval timber bridges had a short life, as the wood decayed quickly and was more easily harmed by floods and ice. The 12th century was an age of economic expansion and the resulting wealth financed the many parish churches of the time. The expertise in construction techniques and craftsmanship, used to build stone churches and castles, was also employed to build stone bridges. For example, a total of 119 stone bridges were constructed in France during the 12th century. The best-known surviving English 12th-century bridge is the Elvet Bridge at Durham, built by the local bishop in 1153–93. There is a saying that London Bridge was built upon woolpacks, which is a reminder that medieval London's wealth was largely based on the export of wool and woollen cloth.

The Knight in the triumph of his heart made several reflections on the greatness of the British Nation: as, that one Englishman could beat three Frenchmen; that we cou'd never be in danger of Popery so long as we took care of our fleet; that the Thames was the noblest river in Europe; that London Bridge was a greater piece of work than any of the Seven Wonders of the World; with many other honest prejudices that naturally cleave to the heart of true Englishman

Joseph Addison, 20 May 1712, *The Spectator*

LEFT Remains of the medieval bridge at Avignon, France, with its chapel

BELOW Elvet Bridge, Durham, showing its surviving medieval chapel; the pointed Gothic-style bridge arches are later replacements

The man who built London Bridge

Peter of Colechurch, a parish priest in the city, is credited with building the stone bridge. He had directed the repair of the timber bridge in 1163, so he was obviously seen as the best person to raise the funds required. Bridge building was viewed as a

ABOVE Young Peter of Colechurch inspecting the bridge building

BELOW Old Peter of Colechurch visiting his bridge

pious, charitable work on a par with church building, another reason a priest was seen as an appropriate person to direct the project. The actual design and construction would have been carried out by master craftsmen, primarily stone masons and carpenters.

Building the stone bridge

Work on the stone bridge is believed to have started in 1176 but, as no record of this event survives, we cannot be certain of the actual date. However, the completion of this momentous project in 1209 was widely recorded. Sadly, Peter of Colechurch died in 1205, four years before the bridge was completed. It is believed that Peter was buried in the crypt below the chapel on his bridge as a tribute to his life's work. Four centuries later, Sir Christopher Wren was similarly buried in the crypt of St Paul's Cathedral, which is generally acknowledged to be both his masterpiece and also his monument.

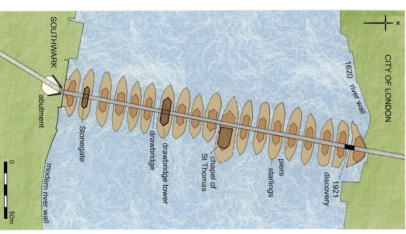

LEFT Plan of the Colechurch bridge showing its major buildings

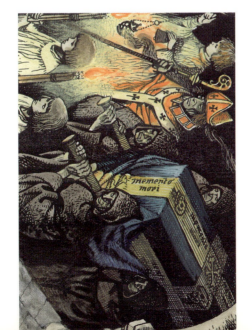

ABOVE The burial of Peter of Colechurch in the bridge chapel

29

The stone bridge was 276 metres (c 906 feet) long with 19 stone arches set on starlings (the 20th was spanned by a drawbridge). The bridge had a large southern abutment, which was built in 1189 or 1190 according to tree-ring dating of its oak foundations. The stone bridge took about 33 years to build – a slow process and one that meant that on average a stone pier was built every 21 months. High river levels during the winter months would have hindered construction, so a lot of the work on the foundations would have been undertaken on a seasonal basis.

Using 19th-century plans produced during demolition of the bridge, we can work out how the piers were constructed without

using cofferdams. First, at low tide, an oval ring of short timber piles would have been driven into the river bed by a human-powered piling machine set up in barges or rafts. Secondly, again at low tide, this enclosure would have been infilled with rubble. Finally, a larger and more powerful piling machine would have been constructed on the infilled enclosure. This machine would have been used to drive in rows of long iron-shod elm piles all around the enclosure. These long piles would have formed a protective barrier (a starling) around the short piles, which could not have withstood the impact of tidal scour, ice flows and floods for long. The gaps amongst these long piles were infilled with rubble and the outermost line of piles further

ABOVE Reconstruction of piling using a barge-borne machine
BELOW General view of medieval London Bridge looking west, showing the Stonegate (left), drawbridge (centre) and chapel (right)

protected by planking. These starlings required endless maintenance to replace piles, as they were constantly being damaged by the daily tides and ice and floods. On top of this consolidated platform, the actual stone pier was constructed.

A temporary wooden framework was erected to support the masonry during construction of the arches between the piers. The stone bridge was clearly a major construction project comparable with the building of a large castle or cathedral.

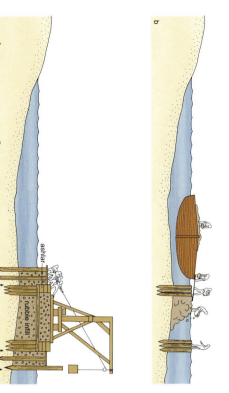

Southwark foreshore

River Thames

natural sand/gravel

N

0 5m

ashlar

rubble infill

pier

starling

LEFT The sequence of bridge pier construction – KEY: a) ring of short piles inserted by a barge-borne machine; b) infilling the pile ring with rubble; c) after placing sillbeams over the infilled area, a large piling engine was set up and used to construct the starling
RIGHT The construction of a masonry bridge pier; the brazier is for heating pitch to seal the joints in the masonry

Shooting the bridge

The rapid flow of water between the closely spaced piers and starlings during the ebb and flow of the tides created a waterfall effect, which obstructed the passage of river craft. Passing through this cascade was known as 'shooting the bridge' and resulted in many a waterman and his passengers drowning. Fifteen people died in 1693 when their boat overturned while passing through the bridge. The hazards of passing under the bridge were immortalised in the proverb 'London Bridge was made for wise men to go over and fools to go under'.

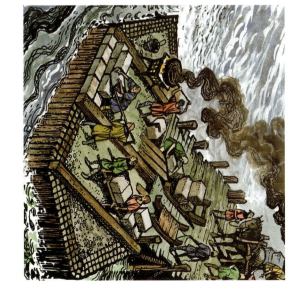

Building the southern abutment

Archaeological excavation in the 1980s revealed the whole plan of the trapezoidal southern bridge abutment. It was beautifully built and all the ashlar blocks were secured with iron clamps set in holes in the top of each block, with the narrow joints between the blocks sealed with pitch. Clearly Peter of Colechurch intended his bridge to last. Construction of the abutment began with dumping soil and flint cobbles to level up the sloping foreshore. Timber piles were driven into the ground and oak beams were laid on top of the piles. The ashlar (faced) masonry that formed the outer sides of the structure was then laid on the beams. Behind the ashlar was a mortared rubble core. The

centre of the completed structure was infilled with clay and chalk rubble, topped by the metalled surface of the sloping approach road. The foreshore on the east or downstream side of the abutment was protected from erosion by a series of wooden revetments. On the upstream side it was protected by a stone wall. The upstream river defences were set further south than the downstream ones, presumably due to the erosion of the foreshore 100 years earlier.

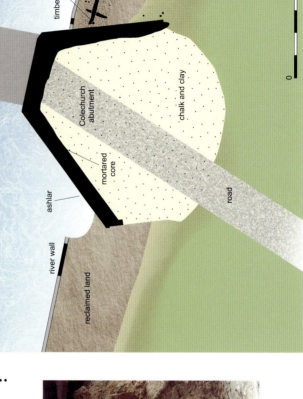

BELOW LEFT The Ragstone ashlar facing blocks of the west side of the Colechurch bridge abutment seen in cross section
BELOW Plan of the Colechurch bridge abutment as revealed in 1984

Maintaining the bridge

London Bridge was maintained with funding from many sources including rent from the houses on the bridge and gifts and bequests from pious Londoners. These bequests included both money and property, which gradually amounted to a substantial landed estate. This was needed to finance the endless maintenance that the bridge and its starlings required. It appears that by 1265 the bridge revenues were being administered by the priests who ran the chapel on the bridge, but by 1284 financial control had passed to the Bridge House Estates, which have now cared for the bridge for centuries. The seal of the Bridge House Estates depicts St Thomas the Martyr in his archbishop's robes standing above one arch of the bridge, with a boat passing through it.

Materials required for bridge maintenance were stored at a yard in Southwark, to the east of St Olaf's church (at Hay's Wharf), which is also thought to be the site of a house belonging to Peter of Colechurch. A 1350 inventory of material in the yard included 400 great pieces of oak, 120 elm piles and a barge. To prevent theft from the Bridge House yard there were several resident guard dogs. The Bridge House weekly accounts refer to 'wages for dogs', presumably the cost of feeding them. Perhaps the wolfish descendants of these dogs guard London scrap yards today.

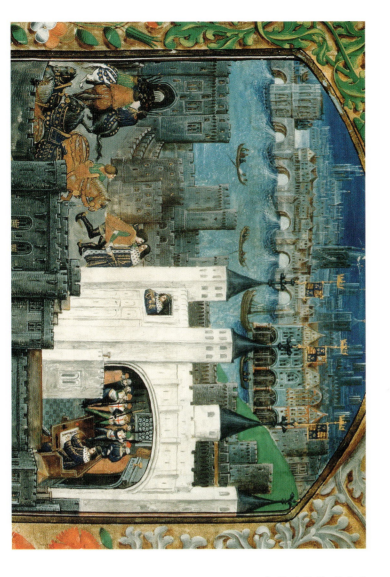

LEFT Earliest known view of medieval London Bridge from an illuminated manuscript of c 1480

RIGHT The Bridge House medieval seal with St Thomas the Martyr on his archbishop's throne on top of the bridge

8 LIVING, DYING AND SHOPPING ON MEDIEVAL LONDON BRIDGE

OLD LONDON BRIDGE (EAST SIDE)

TRAITORS GATE

BELOW London Bridge in c 1630, reconstructed elevation

To London Bridge then rode our King,
The processions there, they met him right,
'Hail England's King' they did sing
'World's flower' they said, God's knight
To London Bridge when he came right,
Upon the gate there stood on high,
A giant that was full grim of sight,
To teach the Frenchmen courtesy

Verse composed to commemorate the triumphant return of Henry V to London on 23 November 1415, after his great victory over the French at the battle of Agincourt

What happened on London bridge

Today bridges are only seen as a quick and easy way of crossing obstacles, but in medieval times urban bridges could also form part of the civic defences or provide sites for housing, shops, chapels and watermills. Medieval London Bridge fulfilled a vast range of functions. It was lined with timber-framed houses and shops, and possessed a chapel dedicated to St Thomas the Martyr as a reminder that bridge building was pious charitable work.

William Chaucer

Thomas Becket, a Londoner, was Archbishop of Canterbury until his murder by four knights in Canterbury Cathedral on 29 December 1170, a deed that was carried out at the instigation of Henry II, with whom he had quarrelled bitterly. People were shocked by his death and he was proclaimed a martyr. His tomb quickly became a major centre of pilgrimage and he was canonised in 1173. The journey of one group of pilgrims from London to Canterbury with the stories they told as entertainment en route is the theme of *The Canterbury tales* by Geoffrey Chaucer (written c 1387–1400).

DRAW BRIDGE

DRAW LOCK

NONESUCH HOUSE

NONESUCH LOCK

CEDAR LOCK

GUT LOCK

LONG ENTRY LOCK

REMAINS OF ST THOMAS'S CHAPEL

CHAPEL LOCK

STATUE OF ST THOMAS A BECKET

LONDON SQUARE

ST MARY'S LOCK

LITTLE LOCK

KINGS LOCK

SHORE LOCK

MILL LOCK

LEFT Reconstruction of the chapel on the bridge c 1500

Many London pilgrims purchased small metal badges as souvenirs and on their return home perhaps threw them off London Bridge into the Thames. One such badge depicts Becket's murder. The chapel was closed in c 1548–9, as part of a national suppression of chantry chapels, and converted into a house. About this time two wooden statues from the chapel may have been thrown into the river by Protestant zealots, who saw sacred images as a breach of one of the Ten Commandments. Centuries later both statues were recovered during dredging. One statue depicts God the Father personified as a pope and the other a Benedictine monk.

ABOVE Medieval pewter badge depicting a bearded pilgrim with a hooded cloak, staff and rosary

RIGHT Medieval wooden statue of a Benedictine monk; found in the Thames

Battles and traitors on London Bridge

The bridge also possessed a 'Stonegate' or barbican and a drawbridge, which defended the city's southern side. The drawbridge allowed the passage of large craft through the bridge but also on five occasions the drawbridge gate served a military function and in 1450 it was the scene of a pitched battle.

On 3 July 1450 Jack Cade and his Kentish rebel army crossed London Bridge unopposed to enter London. Anarchy broke out. Shakespeare vividly described the situation in *Henry VI*, part 2 (act 4, scene 4), with the words 'Jack Cade hath gotten London Bridge; the citizens fly and forsake their houses'.

On the night of 5 July forces composed of the Tower of London garrison and Londoners led by Lord Scales and Captain Matthew Gough recaptured the bridge. The rebels, realising that their success depended on controlling the bridge, immediately counter-attacked. Despite heavy fighting they were unable to take the bridge, so a truce was agreed. Two days later the rebels were

offered a general pardon and returned home except for Cade and the ringleaders, who were arrested and convicted of treason. After execution their decapitated heads were displayed on the top of the Drawbridge Tower as a grisly warning to others.

ABOVE Depiction of William Wallace in full armour

RIGHT Reconstruction of the Drawbridge Gate; notice the decapitated heads of traitors displayed on poles

LEFT AND ABOVE The Wallace monument at Smithfield, London, near the site of his execution

RIGHT 18th-century engraving of the woman in the cage on London Bridge

The first decapitated individual to end up on the Drawbridge Tower had been Sir William Wallace – the Scottish patriot and soldier, who was executed at nearby Smithfield on 23 August 1305. The punishment for treason was gruesome. The convicted traitor was dragged to the place of execution, hung by the neck, then cut down when he was almost dead, only to be disembowelled and have his entrails burnt. He was then decapitated and his body divided into four parts for dispatch to other parts of the kingdom as a grim reminder of the fate that awaited traitors. Wallace's right arm was displayed on the bridge at Newcastle-upon-Tyne, his left arm at Berwick, his right leg at Perth, and his left one at Aberdeen. The earliest monument in Scotland to be erected in memory of Wallace, in 1810 at Wallacestone, stood near the site of the battle of Falkirk (where on 22 July 1298 the English and Welsh army defeated the Scots led by Wallace), and is reputed to include one of the balusters from 18th-century London Bridge.

The practice of displaying the heads of traitors on London Bridge only ended in 1661, the last head being that of the anarchist Thomas Venner.

People were also imprisoned in a 'cage' on London Bridge as a punishment for minor offences. The best known prisoner was a woman, placed here in April 1555 to 'cool herself' for refusing to pray at the nearby church of St Magnus the Martyr for the soul of the recently deceased Pope Julius III. She claimed in her defence that the pious Pope surely did not need her prayers.

Fishing, milling and pageantry on London Bridge

Fish were netted from the bridge and, from 1580, waterwheels were constructed within some arches to power corn mills and extract drinking water from the Thames. Tolls and taxes were collected on the bridge too. The earliest documented instance of this practice dates from c 1000 when it was recorded in a law code that 'a merchant who came up to the bridge with a boat containing fish paid one half-penny as toll and for a large ship one penny'.

London Bridge was also a symbol of civic power and authority; it was the scene of pageants and royal entrances to London. When Henry V returned home in 1415, London Bridge was decorated as the capital's salute to him as the victor of Agincourt (see verse at start of chapter). On top of the towers flanking the Stonegate were two gigantic statues, one of a sentinel holding a battleaxe and the keys of the city, and the other a bejewelled female figure. All around the statues banners and flags fluttered, while 'trumpets, clarions and horns sounded in various melody'. On top of two wooden columns on the bridge approach were the figures of an antelope and a lion, holding the royal arms and the royal standard. The king and his retinue stopped to admire the sight and sounds of their welcome. Then the king called out 'Hail to the royal city!' and rode forwards. The bridge was decorated again in 1421 when Henry returned with his bride Princess Katherine of France.

On St George's day (23 April) 1390, two armoured and mounted knights, Lord Welles and Sir David le Lindesay, had a joust on the bridge in the presence of Richard II. The joust ended with Lord Welles being dismounted and injured.

ABOVE Portrait of Henry V

LEFT The tower housing the London Bridge waterworks at the north end of the bridge in c 1600

RIGHT Braun and Hogenburg's 1572 map of London, with London Bridge and many boats on the river

Houses and shops on London Bridge

It is believed that the stone bridge was lined with houses from the first and in 1281 it was noted that many people were dwelling on the bridge. The main reason for allowing houses on the bridge was their ability to generate income for maintenance. Many medieval bridges, including those at Bristol and Newcastle-Upon-Tyne, were lined with houses. The concept of living on bridges went out of fashion in the 18th century and now only a few examples, such as the Ponte Vecchio in Florence and the 14th-century 'inner bridge' at Esslingen in Germany, survive today. Pennant described the trials of living on London Bridge in 1813: 'Nothing but use could preserve the repose of the innates, who soon grew deaf to the noise of

the falling waters, the clamors of the watermen or the frequent shrieks of drowning wretches.'

Despite being cramped, shops and inns on the bridge fetched high rents, as there was a lot of 'passing trade' from pedestrians. Attempts to make these timber-framed properties as large as possible meant that by the 16th century they were up to four or five storeys high. Sometimes, at upper floor level, extra rooms were gained by building across the central roadway. Sanitation was provided by sentry box-like privies built out over the river, which could have caused some unpleasant surprises for those passing under the bridge in small boats.

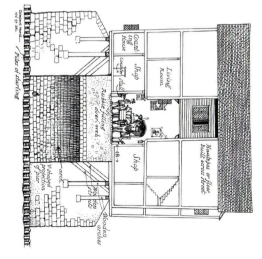

ABOVE *Houses on Bristol bridge*

LEFT *Bridge at Esslingen, Germany, with its chapel and shops built on the bridge piers*

RIGHT *Cross section of medieval London Bridge, showing the structure and size of the houses*

Medieval finds contemporary with the houses on the bridge were recovered during dredging work in 1824–41. They appear to have been inadvertently dropped or perhaps intentionally thrown into the river. Finds include pottery vessels, iron axe heads, bronze fish hooks, coins, a crucifix, pins,

RIGHT *Copper-alloy pin from London Bridge*

BELOW *Gold finger ring with garnet cabochon from London Bridge*

ABOVE *Part of the handle of a 13th-century London ware jug depicting a human face; found on a waterfront site just upstream from London Bridge*

RIGHT *A late 15th-century diamond knop spoon made of lead; recovered from reclaimed land near London Bridge*

A rental survey of *c* 1358 shows that there were 62 shops on the east side of the roadway and 69 on the west side. Inns on the bridge after 1600 included the Anchor and Crown, the Angel, the Blue Boar, the Golden Globe, and the Lock of Hair. Inns on the southern approach road included the Bear and Dolphin taverns: the medieval and later foundations of these two properties were found during the excavation of the bridge abutment. During the 17th century two landlords of the Bear, Abraham Browne and Cornelius Cooke, issued their own tokens or private money.

ABOVE *17th-century tokens issued by Browne and Cook(e), publicans at the Bear on the Bridge Foot*

three signet rings, daggers, spoons, keys and padlocks. On the foreshore near the southern bridge abutment, a medieval gold finger ring set with a garnet was found. People are still throwing things off the modern bridge into the river – during 1967 dredging around the modern bridge revealed a number of unwanted military revolvers and knuckledusters. Post-medieval muzzle-loading cannons have also been recovered during dredging downstream of the bridge and were presumably lost or jettisoned from sailing ships visiting the port of London.

It was not just objects that fell into the river – the residents of the bridge sometimes fell out of their houses into the river too. In 1536 Anne Hewett, the young daughter of wealthy cloth maker Sir William Hewett (died 1567), fell from their house on the bridge into the river. She was rescued by one of her father's apprentices, Edward Osborne (died 1591). Edward later married Anne and they had five children. He enjoyed a very successful career as a cloth maker, becoming both Lord Mayor (1583–4) and a Sheriff of London.

ABOVE Portrait of Sir William Hewett

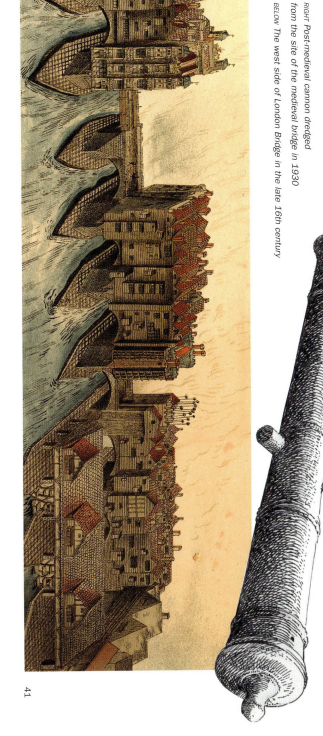

RIGHT Post-medieval cannon dredged from the site of the medieval bridge in 1930

BELOW The west side of London Bridge in the late 16th century

Frost fairs and skating

The ice which could destroy the bridge during very cold winters sometimes built up upstream of the bridge. This allowed frost fairs to be held on the ice several times between 1607 and 1814. In 1684 the attractions included bull baiting, roasting oxen and football matches; printing presses set up on the ice sold souvenir tickets to visitors with their names specially printed on them. The closely placed piers and starlings, which acted as a partial dam, would have greatly encouraged the build-up of ice on the upstream side of the bridge.

People also skated on the ice and evidence of medieval bone ice skates has been found on various excavations in London. Fitz Stephen, writing in c 1170–83 about the pastimes of Londoners, noted that some people skated on the frozen marshes of Moorfields, north of the walled city: they 'fit to their feet the shin-bones of beasts, lashing them beneath their ankles, and with iron-shod poles in their hands they strike ever and anon against the ice and are borne along swift as a bird in flight ...'

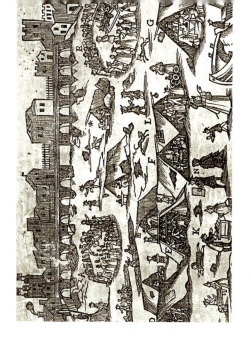

ABOVE Frost fair on the Thames in 1715, view looking east towards the bridge

BELOW Frost fair card, printed on the ice as a souvenir in 1684

HENRY, Earl of Clarendon,
FLORA, Countess of Clarendon.
EDWARD, Lord Cornbury.

London: Printed by G.Croom, on the ICE,
on the River of Thames, February 2. 1684

ABOVE View of the frozen Thames and medieval London Bridge looking east, by Hondius 1677, showing area of housing on the bridge destroyed by the Great Fire

FAR LEFT Bone skate from London Bridge foreshore

LEFT Boy ice skating on bone skates, propelling himself along with two iron-tipped poles

9 LONDON BRIDGE IS 'BROKEN DOWN'

London Bridge is broken down,

Broken Down, broken down,

London Bridge is broken down,

My fair lady

Anon

Above right is the first verse of the famous English nursery rhyme of unknown antiquity but there is no firm evidence to suggest which collapse of the bridge this refers to. The 'lady' in question may, however, have been Eleanor of Provence, queen to Henry III (1216–72), who had custody of the funds intended to maintain the bridge, which she misspent, contributing to the collapse of five arches of the bridge during the severe winter of 1281–2. This collapse prompted the Queen to return responsibility for the bridge to the Londoners for them to repair. In February 1282 the mayor and the wealthier citizens of London contributed money towards the cost of building a temporary bridge, on the understanding that parliament would repay the money and fund the subsequent rebuilding.

© Dean and Chapter of Westminster

LEFT Henry III's tomb effigy, Westminster Abbey

Why did the bridge collapse?

A serious design fault was the main reason the bridge could quickly become derelict and collapse. Its piers were not constructed within cofferdams, which would have allowed them to rest on solid geology, in contrast to the Trier bridge for example (Chapter 3). Instead the piers were founded on shallow pile foundations and only protected from the scouring effects of the tides and flood waters by concentric lines of long elm piles sheathed in planking and infilled with rubble (Chapter 7). If these starlings were not constantly maintained they were simply washed away, allowing the current to erode the foundations of the pier, causing the masonry to subside and crack. During very cold weather, when ice formed on the river, the expansion in volume caused by water freezing within the larger cracks was enough to tear the masonry apart.

After the problems of 1282, Londoners ensured that they always kept control of their bridge. From 1381 onwards an almost unbroken sequence of accounts and records relating to London Bridge and its maintenance survives as part of the Bridge House Estates. These include records of the payments of wages to labourers and tradesman, the purchase of timber and building stone, and the record of rents from the various properties owned by Bridge House. Today the Bridge House Estates, administered by the Corporation of London, have become a charity, which not only maintains the four City of London road bridges but also funds various good causes.

The collapse of 1437 and its aftermath

From 1282 until the 1420s there is no evidence of any serious problems with the maintenance of the bridge; in fact the Bridge House records confirm that its starlings were constantly maintained. This state of affairs changed in January 1425 when an examination of the southern arches of the bridge around the Stonegate revealed cracks in the masonry. The situation was serious enough for heavy carts to be banned from crossing the bridge. In July 1435 it was noted that the bridge had fallen into a ruinous condition. The reasons for this situation are unclear but it is possible that money was being misused or embezzled and

that shoddy workmanship and materials may have contributed to the problem. Between 5 and 12 January 1437 a huge build-up of ice around the bridge piers caused the Stonegate and its two adjoining arches to collapse. A large stone corbel decorated with a human head, found during dredging on the site, may have formed part of the Stonegate.

The collapse would have caused immediate problems to trade and the capital's food supply, as the nearest upstream bridge was at Kingston and there were no bridges downstream. Ferrying everything across the river would have been time-consuming and expensive, and the Bridge House Estates needed to get the bridge repaired immediately. They sent to Canterbury for Richard Beke, then clerk of works in charge of cathedral maintenance, who had been chief mason in charge of the maintenance of London Bridge (1417–35). He was clearly the right man for the job: according to the Bridge House records he quickly started building a temporary wooden bridge across the starlings. By 9 March 30 carpenters were working on the construction of the temporary bridge, which was completed by the end of the month. Richard Beke and the chief carpenter were paid large bonuses for their efforts.

Rebuilding the southern abutment

The collapse of 1437 prompted a huge amount of rebuilding work. Over the next 35 years, and arch by arch, the whole bridge was rebuilt on a piecemeal basis and the Stonegate completely rebuilt. As part of this great rebuilding the southern abutment, which had not been damaged by the 1437 collapse and showed no sign of structural failure, was enlarged. This rebuilding probably took place in 1445–60.

Work on the abutment started with consolidation of the muddy tidal foreshore. This was achieved by driving in hundreds of closely spaced iron-shod elm piles into the ground adjoining the north-west corner of the 12th-century abutment. Sill beams for the new wall were laid along the edge of the piles. A wall of Kentish Ragstone ashlar blocks was constructed on the sill beams. All the blocks were secured by iron clamps set

in hot lead and the joints between the blocks sealed by bitumen. A mass of mortar and rubble was poured behind the ashlar. New up- and downstream river walls were constructed at about the same time. A small landing place was established on the upstream side for the use of maintenance men when they travelled out to the starlings by boat.

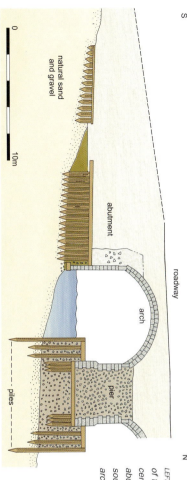

LEFT Cross section of the 15th-century bridge abutment and southernmost arch of bridge

roadway

N

ABOVE Mass of elm piles used to consolidate the foreshore adjoining the north-west corner of the 12th-century bridge abutment

ABOVE LEFT Ashlar facing of the west side of the enlarged 15th-century bridge abutment

BELOW Plan of the enlarged 15th-century bridge abutment, showing relationship to the earlier abutment

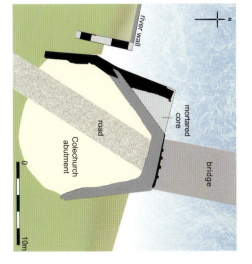

N

river wall

road

mortared core

bridge

Colechurch abutment

0   10m

The 'golden age' of London Bridge

After the great rebuilding of the bridge arches, many of the houses on the bridge were also rebuilt. One such rebuilding is witnessed by the discovery of a stone carved with the date 1509, found during the 1758 modification of the bridge. The bridge was seen as a lucrative place to have shop or business premises on account of the huge volume of traffic that came past.

Many historians and travellers recorded their eyewitness impressions of the bridge. Mancini, writing in 1482–3, described it as 'a famous bridge built partly of wood and partly of stone. On it there are houses and several gates with portcullises; the dwelling houses are built above the workshops and belong to diverse sorts of craftsmen.'

At about the same time people started to illustrate the bridge. Wyngaerde produced the first complete representation in c 1544 as part of his London panorama. In 1559 the now redundant Drawbridge Tower was demolished and replaced by a large timber-framed house, which resembled a castle keep with its four turreted corner towers.

ABOVE *Stone inscribed with date 1509, found during demolition of houses on London Bridge in 1758*

ABOVE *Bone handle decorated with bears or baboons from London Bridge*

LEFT *Model of 16th-century London Bridge, view looking west*

The inns and taverns around the bridge certainly attracted some wealthy customers or criminals – when the Bear tavern on the southern approach to the bridge was being demolished in 1761, 'three pots' full of Elizabethan (1558–1603) gold and silver coins were apparently found. People carried on dropping or throwing things into the river as before, including a bone knife handle decorated with bears or baboon-like creatures.

The good life on the bridge was soon to be interrupted again, this time by fire not ice. On the night of 11 February 1633, a fire broke out in a house near the church of St Magnus (adjoining the northern side of the bridge) and the following day the fire spread to the north end of the bridge itself, destroying 42 houses. Sir Anthony Van Dyke was living nearby at his studio within the precinct of London Blackfriars (south of modern Ludgate Hill) and may have been inspired to record this dramatic event from the vantage point of his upstream studio. Fire returned to the bridge on 2 September 1666, when the notorious Great Fire of London, which destroyed some 85% of the medieval city, burnt the newly replaced buildings on the northern end of the bridge.

ABOVE The fire on the north end of the bridge during the night of 11 February 1633; painting possibly produced in the studio of Van Dyke (detail)

BELOW Painting of Great Fire of London (Dutch school c 1666) with the bridge to the left

10 LONDON BRIDGE IN DECLINE

The 'keep left' rule and London Bridge

An increasing problem with medieval London Bridge was that its roadway was only c 3.6–4.6 metres wide (c 12 to 15 feet), making it barely wide enough for two large carts or coaches to pass each other. The narrow roadway and the absence of pavements made crossing the bridge hazardous to pedestrians, who could only cross safely by walking behind a large vehicle. After the 1633 fire destroyed the buildings on the northern end of the bridge, it was proposed to widen the roadway by about 1 metre (3 feet). Samuel Pepys, the diarist, on 24

January 1666, described the impact of gale-force winds on the fire-damaged portion of the bridge: 'all the pales [wooden posts] of London-Bridge on both sides were blown away, so that we were fain [forced] to stoop very low for fear of blowing off the bridge.'

After the Great Fire of September 1666 the buildings on the northern end of the bridge were again rebuilt and the opportunity was taken in 1685 to further widen this portion of the roadway to 6 metres (c 20 feet). In 1728 the Stonegate was rebuilt and its arch was also widened to improve traffic flow.

RIGHT London Bridge c 1560, a view from Southwark

BELOW Norden's engraving of London Bridge c 1600, looking west

In 1722 a series of tolls were introduced for carts and wagons using the bridge, and the Court of Common Council ordered that, to prevent obstructions, three persons be appointed to direct approaching traffic to the left side of the approach way. This is the first recorded instance of traffic management in England and of the 'keep left' rule now enshrined in *The highway code*. Why this particular side of the road was chosen is uncertain. It has been suggested that the left side was chosen because swords are worn on the left side and drawn with the right arm, but this seems implausible as swords were not widely worn outside court and military

circles. By the 18th century many English wagon drivers sat on the right side of their vehicles so they could more easily see the position of their vehicle relative to oncoming traffic on the right-hand side. There is also a long-standing tradition in England of leading and mounting a horse on the left side.

Traffic management and widening of the roadway was clearly not enough to cope with the ever-increasing volume of traffic using the bridge. In spring 1749, after a public rehearsal of Handel's *Music for the royal fireworks* in Vauxhall Gardens, the extra traffic the crowds generated blocked the bridge for three hours.

LEFT The last Stonegate, built in 1728

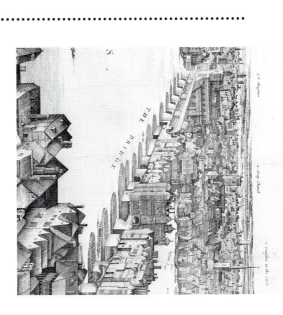

ABOVE Hollar's view of London Bridge after the 1633 fire, showing the palisaded gap at the north end

BELOW Buck's 1749 view of London Bridge still lined with houses

49

Westminster Bridge

Until the construction of a bridge at Putney in 1729, Kingston Bridge was the nearest upstream crossing to London Bridge, although the river was crossed by ferries. By the 17th century the continual expansion of London and Westminster was generating ever more road traffic. Pressure mounted for the construction of a new bridge at Westminster to relieve traffic congestion. In 1664, the Corporation of London, who bribed Charles II to oppose the project, scuppered this proposal. In 1738 construction of a new bridge at Westminster finally began. The work, which was not completed until 1750, was a series of disasters from start to finish. To begin with Parliament attempted to fund the construction of the bridge by state lottery. The lottery proved to be fraudulent, with multiple winning tickets, and had to be abandoned. To save money the piers were not built inside cofferdams but instead their foundations were sunk into dredged holes in the river bed. The shallow foundations suffered from subsidence and scouring. This was so bad that several piers had be rebuilt and strengthened before the bridge could be completed; hence the popular nickname 'the bridge of fools'. In 1862 the bridge was demolished due to persistent structural problems and a new one built.

Composed upon Westminster Bridge

Westminster Bridge inspired William Wordsworth on 3 September 1802 to compose the following. Since November 2003, Wordsworth's poem is commemorated with a plaque on the bridge.

Earth has not any thing to shew more fair:
Dull would he be of soul who could pass by
A sight so touching in its majesty:
This City now doth like a garment wear
The beauty of the morning: silent, bare,
Ships, towers, domes, theatres, and temples lie
Open unto the fields, and to the sky;
All bright and glittering in the smokeless air.
Never did sun more beautifully steep
In his first splendour valley, rock, or hill;
Ne'er saw I, never felt, a calm so deep!
The river glideth at his own sweet will:
Dear God! the very houses seem asleep;
And all that mighty heart is lying still!

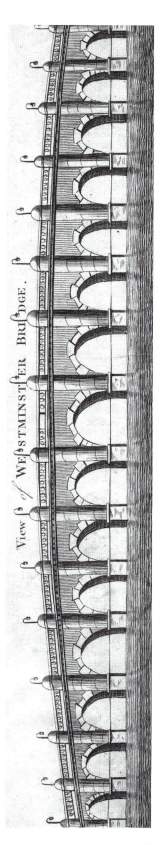

BELOW Engraving of Westminster Bridge

The modification of old London Bridge

Westminster Bridge, despite its design flaws, was a great improvement on London Bridge as its roadway was much wider (it was not lined with houses) and it possessed pavements. The large arches of Westminster Bridge also allowed the easy movement of river craft. There were not sufficient funds available to rebuild London Bridge, so it was decided in 1756 to modify the old bridge instead.

Between 1757 and 1762, the architects George Dance and Roger Taylor transformed medieval London Bridge into a wider and modern-looking structure. The work involved demolishing all the buildings on the bridge and then widening the structure by extending each side on top of the starlings. The widened bridge was faced with ashlar blocks of Portland stone. Widening of the bridge created a 10m (33ft) roadway, flanked by pavements. To improve navigation and water-flow the central pier and starling was removed, and replaced in 1759 by the 'great arch'. The widened bridge was also furnished with baroque-style balustrades, streetlights and 14 alcoves built on alternate piers. One of these alcoves now stands in the grounds of Guy's Hospital. Iron railings removed at this time from the small area of open space on the old bridge, known as the Square, were reused in the churchyard of St Botolph's, Bishopsgate, in the City of London.

While the widening of London Bridge was being carried out, traffic crossed via a temporary wooden bridge built across the starlings on the western side of the bridge. This temporary bridge burnt down on 11 April 1758. It was claimed that the fire was the result of arson and armed men guarded the replacement temporary bridge.

11 RENNIE'S LONDON BRIDGE

... the spoiling influences of water – discoloured copper, rotten wood, honeycombed stone, green dank deposit ...

Dickens' description of the effect of the London Thames in *Our mutual friend*

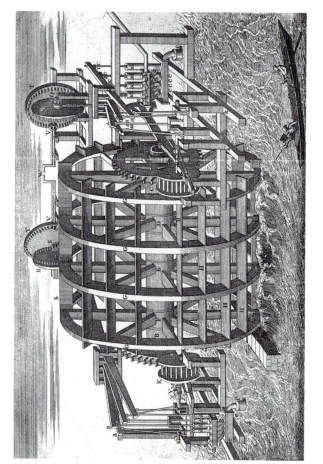

LEFT *The silent highwayman, a Tenniel cartoon illustrating the appalling state of the Thames in 1858*

BELOW *The gearing of the London Bridge waterworks in 1749*

As London continued to expand during the 18th century, there was pressure to build more Thames bridges and so more bridges were built – at Blackfriars (1760–9), Waterloo (1811–17) and Southwark (1814–19). A traffic census records that on one day, in July 1811, 89,640 pedestrians, 2924 carts and drays, 1240 coaches, 769 wagons and 764 horses and gigs and taxed carts passed over London Bridge. Now about 38,000 vehicles cross London Bridge every day.

As London expanded, more and more raw sewage was poured into the Thames, grossly polluting the river. As many Londoners relied on the Thames for drinking water, this situation resulted in repeated outbreaks of cholera and other diseases. From 1580 to 1822 drinking water was extracted from the Thames at London Bridge, initially by tidal water wheels (set in the arches of the bridge), which powered hydraulic pumps. From 1786 water was extracted using a steam engine to drive an atmospheric pump.

The construction of the Rennie bridge

By the 1820s London Bridge was in poor repair and there was growing pressure to improve navigation to allow the Port of London to expand upstream of the bridge. The old bridge was also damaged in the severe winter of 1813–14, when the river was frozen for a long period of time and the last frost fair was held. It was decided to build a completely new bridge and approach roads, alongside the old one, rather than try to rebuild the old bridge. On the north bank a completely new approach road – King William Street – was to be laid out, running from the Royal Exchange to the new bridge. On the south side, the existing bridge approach road, Borough High Street, was to be realigned and widened. Work on the new

bridge started on 15 March 1824, and the foundation stone was laid on 15 June 1825.

The Portland ashlar stone piers of the new five-arch bridge were constructed inside huge timber cofferdams pumped dry by steam engines. The new bridge was designed and built by John Rennie and his two sons George and John. After Rennie's death in 1821, his younger son John took over as chief engineer; in recognition of his achievement in completing the bridge, he was knighted in 1831. William IV opened the new bridge on 1 August 1831. It had taken seven years and seven months to build and had cost £2,556,170, inclusive of the cost of building the new approach roads and demolishing the old bridge.

ABOVE The Lord Mayor's procession passing under the unfinished arches of new London Bridge, 9 November 1827

BELOW The opening of London Bridge by William IV in 1831

BELOW LEFT Timber-framed shops and houses in Borough High Street demolished during the widening of the bridge approach road in Southwark

53

The demolition of old London Bridge

The demolition of old London Bridge in 1831–2 sparked the first awareness of the historical value of what was being destroyed. There was brisk trade in producing snuff boxes, eggcups and other trinkets, and even items of furniture including tables and chairs made out of fragments of the starling timbers. Dredging around the site of the bridge in 1824–41 revealed thousands of Roman and medieval coins and other antiquities. Charles Roach Smith purchased many of these objects from the dredger crews who found them. Roach Smith was a great collector of London antiquities and opened a 'Museum of London Antiquities' to display his finds to the public, until he sold his collection to the British Museum in 1856. These finds became the nucleus of the British Museum's Roman and medieval collections.

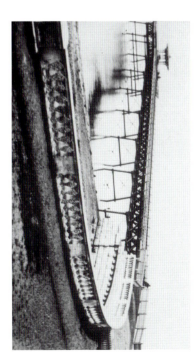

The remains of Peter of Colechurch, the builder of the 12th-century London Bridge, had lain undisturbed in his tomb below the floor of the lower storey of the former chapel on the bridge for centuries. His bones were probably rediscovered during the demolition of the bridge and it seems that they were just tipped into the river. This was a sad end for a great man and contrasts with that of his contemporary Bénézet (died 1184), who started the construction of the great French bridge at Avignon in c 1177–8. Bénézet was buried in the chapel on his bridge and made a saint. Recent examination of the bones in a casket in the collections of the Museum of London, reputed to be those of Colechurch, revealed that only one of the bones is human and the rest are animal, suggesting that this is a bogus relic.

When old London Bridge was 'broken down' for the last time, after some 622 years, this was not the end of it. The canny demolition contractors sold off much of the ashlar. Two of the bridge's alcoves have stood in Victoria Park, east London, since 1860 and a third in the grounds of Guy's Hospital since 1861. Some ashlar blocks from the modified 18th-century bridge were used to face Ingress Abbey at Greenhithe in Kent (built 1832–3), the home of James Harmer (1777–1853), a wealthy City of London alderman, lawyer and newspaper owner. Other ashlar blocks were used to build a barge quay at Beaumont in Essex. Part of the balustrade was used on the approach to Herne Bay pier until it was swept away by the great 1953 east coast storm. In 1836 the church tower of St James Warden, on the Isle of Sheppey in Kent, was rebuilt with stone from the demolished bridge but sadly, due to coastal erosion, the church was demolished in 1876. Other fragments may well exist in surprising places around Britain and their discovery would add to the story of old London Bridge.

12 NEW LONDON BRIDGE AND ITS CONTEMPORARIES

In 1894 Tower Bridge was opened – a new downstream crossing whose drawbridge would allow the Port of London to function. Its roadway divides into two parts that are lifted hydraulically by engines housed in its twin gothic towers. There is a high-level walkway for pedestrians, which was originally used when the bridge was raised. This famous bridge came 34th in a 2004 survey of distinctive symbols of Britain.

On 21 June 1921, King George V opened the newly rebuilt Southwark Bridge.

Sir John Rennie's London Bridge was widened in 1913, to accommodate a four-lane roadway. Despite this change, in the 1960s it was decided to replace it with a much wider bridge that would cope better with the ever-increasing volume of traffic and pedestrians. In 1967–71 Rennie's bridge was dismantled and replaced by a new three-arch bridge with pre-stressed concrete cantilevers and a six-lane roadway: 'three slender spans, founded on concrete piers dug deep into the clay. Short stone masts stand on the cutwaters' (Bradley and Pevsner 1997). Elizabeth II opened the new bridge on 16 March 1973.

Unreal City,
Under the brown fog of a winter dawn,
A crowd flowed over London Bridge, so many,
I had not thought death had undone so many

T S Eliot 1922, The waste land

ABOVE *New London Bridge today, looking north towards Adelaide House where part of the medieval bridge was found in 1921*

FAR LEFT *The opening of Southwark Bridge in 1921*

LEFT *London Bridge in 1909, a view westwards towards Southwark Cathedral*

The ashlar facing from Rennie's bridge was sold to the MacCulloch Oil Company for some £1,025,000. The bridge was rebuilt stone by stone at Lake Havasu City, Arizona, as a tourist attraction, spanning part of Lake Havasu. This rebuilt bridge was opened in 1971. Urban folklore suggests the Americans thought they were buying Tower Bridge.

New bridges continue to be needed. The Queen Elizabeth II Bridge across the River Thames at Dartford, Kent, was opened in October 1991 and intended to relieve congestion at the Dartford Tunnel. It is the lowest bridge crossing the estuary. This cable-stayed high-level toll bridge was built at a cost of £184 million. With a total length of 2.8km, it is one of the longest bridges of its type in Europe. Over 40 million vehicles cross it each year. In February 2004 it was decided to proceed with the new Thames Gateway Bridge, to link Beckton and Thamesmead; it is expected to cost £450 million and should be completed by 2013.

Within the City of London the latest bridge to be constructed is the 325 metre-long, steel Millennium Bridge, a footbridge linking Tate Modern art gallery with St Paul's Cathedral. It opened on 10 June 2001, but closed shortly afterwards due to excessive

swaying; after modifications it reopened on 27 February 2002. London's newest bridge is actually two footbridges, flanking Charing Cross rail bridge. The bridges, named the Golden Jubilee Bridges in commemoration of the 50th anniversary of the Queen's accession, were opened on 2 July 2003 and are generally known as the Hungerford Bridge. The story of bridging the Thames is certainly not complete.

ABOVE London Bridge at Lake Havasu, Arizona

ABOVE RIGHT The Millennium Bridge

RIGHT The proposed design of Thamesmead Bridge

13 WHERE TO SEE OLD LONDON BRIDGE TODAY

Sweet Thames, run softly, till I end my Song

Spencer

A preserved alcove from the 18th-century modifications to the London Bridge can be found in the grounds of Guy's Hospital, Southwark, London SE1; two more such alcoves can be seen in Victoria Park, Hackney, London E3.

Outside the church of St Magnus, Lower Thames Street, London EC3, there are a few *ex situ* Portland ashlar blocks from the 18th-century modifications to the bridge. These blocks are believed to be from the portion of the bridge discovered and destroyed during the construction of nearby Adelaide House in 1921–2. On display inside the church of St Magnus is a model of the 15th-century bridge.

The last set of royal arms of George II (1727–60) from the Stonegate is now reset in the facade of the King's Arms public house, Newcomen Street, Southwark. The arms were altered to those of George III (1760–1820), probably in 1787.

At Beaumont Quay, to the north of Thorpe-le-Soken, near Clapton-on-Sea, Essex, a barge quay was constructed in 1833 from

blocks of Portland ashlar facing, all dating from the 18th-century modifications to the bridge. The quay, which was built as a speculative venture by the Trustees of Guy's Hospital, was a commercial failure as competition from the railways finished the movement of bulk cargoes by coastal sailing barge by the 1860s.

ABOVE Beaumont Quay, near Thorpe-le-Soken, Essex
LEFT Royal arms of George III in the facade of the King's Arms public house, Newcomen Street, Southwark

The reconstructed Rennie's London Bridge has been on display at Lake Havasu City, Arizona, in the United States of America, since 1971. The largest remaining portion of Rennie's bridge in London is the Portland ashlar facing in the Southwark approach and abutment. This is best viewed from the Tooley Street arch which passes through the abutment. To the west of the Rennie abutment (outside the Mud Lark public house, Tooley Street) are six granite blocks from the Rennie bridge brought from Hay's Wharf in 1977. The stairs on the west side of the Southwark abutment are the setting of Nancy's meeting with Mr Brownlow and Rose Maylie in Dickens' novel *Oliver Twist* (chapter

BELOW The London Bridge alcove in the grounds of Guy's Hospital

46). Nancy informs them of Oliver's whereabouts; unfortunately they are secretly overheard by Noah Claypole, an event which results in the murder of Nancy.

The Museum of London, London Wall, London EC2, exhibits a wide range of material relating to the capital's history from the prehistoric to the present day. Displays include prehistoric finds from the Thames and information on the Roman port, while there is a small display about the bridge and

the Viking-age weapons found near the bridge in the medieval gallery. Several famous paintings of the bridge and the portrait of Sir William Hewett are also exhibited in the museum.

The Museum in Docklands, West India Quay, London E1, exhibits (on floor 3) more material relating to the medieval London Bridge, including two splendid models of the bridge showing its appearance in *c* 1440 and *c* 1600.

LEFT The Museum in Docklands

FURTHER READING

Ayre, J, and Wroe-Brown, R, 2002 *The London Millennium Bridge: excavation of the medieval and later waterfronts at Peter's Hill, City of London, and Bankside, Southwark*, MoLAS Archaeol Stud Ser 6, London

Bradley, S, and Pevsner, N, 1997 *The buildings of England: London 1, the City of London*, London (for descriptions of modern bridges)

Cowan, C, 1998 *Below Southwark: the archaeological story*, London

Currie, I, 1996 *Frosts, freezes and fairs*, London

Harding, V, and Wright, L (eds), 1995 *London Bridge: selected accounts and rentals, 1381–1538*, London Rec Soc 31, London

Harrison, D, 2004 *The bridges of medieval England: transport and society 400–1800*, Oxford

Hewett, D, in prep *Sir William Hewett 1496–1566/7 Lord Mayor of London* (privately published)

Home, G C, 1931 *Old London Bridge*, London (very good, but never reprinted so hard to find)

Jackson, P, 2002 *London Bridge: a visual history*, London (fully revised edition of his 1971 book with lots of original illustrations)

Pierce, P, 2001 *Old London Bridge*, London

Milne, G, 1993 *The port of Roman London* (2 edn), London (see Chapter 4 for the Roman bridge)

Rowsome, P, 2000 *Heart of the city: Roman, medieval and modern London revealed by archaeology at 1 Poultry*, London

Swanton, M J (ed), 1996 *The Anglo-Saxon chronicle*, London

Thomas, C, 2002 *The archaeology of medieval London*, Stroud

Walker, R J B, 1979 *Old Westminster Bridge – the bridge of fools*, Newton Abbot

Watson, B, Brigham, T, and Dyson, T, 2001 *London bridge: 2000 years of a river crossing*, MoLAS Monogr 8, London

Music

Eric Coates wrote a march entitled 'London Bridge'

Websites

www.museumoflondon.org.uk
Museum of London, 150 London Wall, London EC2

www.museumindocklands.org.uk
Museum in Docklands, No. 1 Warehouse, West India Quay, Hertsmere Road, London E1

www.cityoflondon.gov.uk\guildhall.artgallery
Guildhall Art Gallery, London EC2 has the largest collection of views of London Bridge, see their on-line collage database for details

www.oldlondonbridge.com
The London Bridge Museum and Educational Trust

www.bridgehousegrants.org.uk
The Bridge House Estates Trust